CW00383123

THE OU.

BENEDICTA WARD SLG

SLG PRESS

Convent of the Incarnation
Fairacres Parker Street
Oxford OX4 1TB England
www.slgpress.co.uk

First published as a contribution to
Joy of Heaven: Springs of Christian Spirituality,
ed. Benedicta Ward and Ralph Waller, SPCK, 2003 (pp. 30-55)

First published as a separate work by SLG Press, 2012

ISBN   978-0-7283-0202-0
ISSN   0307-1405

Printed by:
Will Print Oxford England

CONTENTS

Cover illustration

The cover photograph, *Eglise Pater Noster*, created by W. Robrecht on 8 March 2007, is licensed by W. Robrecht under the:

Creative Commons Attribution-Share Alike 3.0 Unported Licence,

so that it may be shared and derivative works made, provided that it is appropriately attributed, and distributed under this or a similar later Creative Commons license or a Creative Commons Compatible Licence, without any suggestion that the author of the image has endorsed the user or the user's use of the work. SLG Press uses and distributes the image under these terms of this licence. Reference may be made to the image and terms via:

http://commons.wikimedia.org/wiki/Main_Page

http://creativecommons.org/licenses/by-sa/3.0/legalcode

INTRODUCTION

Our Father, who art in heaven,
hallowed be thy name.
Thy kingdom come.
Thy will be done on earth as it is in heaven.
Give us this day our daily bread.
And forgive us our trespasses,
as we forgive those who trespass against us.
And lead us not into temptation,
but deliver us from evil. Amen.

In the Gospels of Matthew (6: 9-13) and of Luke (11: 2-4) we read that the disciples said to Jesus, 'Lord, teach us to pray.' His response, 'When you pray, say, "Our Father, who art in heaven"', has created the best-known of all Christian texts, the Our Father. In Greek, or in translation into Latin, or in the many forms of the vernacular languages, it is a point of unity between all using it, and therefore it is important that the words remain as unchanged as possible. It has been seen as the teaching of the Lord himself about prayer and has been known by innumerable people, who have used it in just that way. Known by heart, the text has become physically part of those praying, and has then continued to act as a gateway into prayer for the whole of their lives without further analysis. That is its purpose, but there is also a place for thinking about the words and for using the intellect to explore their riches. There are, therefore, countless commentaries on each section of it. This exploration has been done by commentators from the early Church until today, and, though there is a basic similarity between them, there is also much that expresses a difference of perception in detail.

1

I have chosen five writers as expositors of this prayer: Origen from the third century; John Cassian from the fourth; two Englishmen, the Venerable Bede and Alcuin of York, from the eighth; and Teresa of Avila from the sixteenth. General comments of each writer about the prayer make up the next section, followed by a section of more detailed reflections on each of the clauses.

GENERAL COMMENTS

Origen

Origen (c. 185-254), the earliest and greatest of the early Church Fathers, wrote his commentary on the Our Father in the form of a letter, which in length seems better described by the word 'treatise', addressed to an elderly friend, Ambrose, and his wife Tatiana.[1] Such personal spiritual instruction has often taken the form of a letter, since, although such texts were meant to be a public type of literature, the more personal use of the first person singular was found to be especially appropriate for spirituality. The whole of Christian prayer was described by Origen in terms of the clauses of the Our Father, and this provided the method for later writers. His commentary was formed by the style of patristic commentary on Scripture: first presenting a literal discussion of the grammar of the text; then asking what it means to the reader; and then what it tells the reader about Christ and about heaven. The whole Bible was seen as a word of God, and all parts were seen to interpret every other part. So in commenting on this key prayer, Origen applied different levels of understanding to each part and also set it within the whole of Scripture. He began with the grammatical and textual aspects of the passage, noticing differences between the two versions as a basis for further discussion:

> I have said enough already about the problem of prayer in general, so I will now go on to the next task, and look at the prayer given by the Lord and the power with which it is filled. First, notice that it only seems that Matthew and Luke have written the same form of prayer according to which we should pray. The words given by Matthew are as follows: Our Father, who art in heaven, hallowed be thy name. Thy kingdom come. Thy will be done on earth as it is in heaven. Give us this day our

3

supersubstantial bread. And forgive us our debts, as we also forgive our debtors. And lead us not into temptation, but deliver us from evil. But Luke reads thus: Father, hallowed be thy name. Thy kingdom come. Give us each day our supersubstantial bread. And forgive us our sins, for we also forgive everyone that is indebted to us. And lead us not into temptation.[2]

After discussing each phrase of the prayer in depth, at the end Origen drew the treatise together with an outline of the shape of Christian prayer as seen in the Our Father:

> I am going to bring this treatise to an end by going through the essential parts of prayer. I have found scattered in the Scriptures four important aspects that need explaining, and all should organize their prayer with these as a pattern. Here are the main parts: at the beginning, at the start of prayer, wholeheartedly glorify God through Christ, who is glorified with him, in the Holy Spirit, who is praised with him. Next, thank God for all his benefits, remembering both those things that are given in general to all and those that are special to you. This thanksgiving, I think, should be followed by a sorrowful confession of sins; ask God first for healing in order to be delivered from customs that lead to sin, and ask then for forgiveness of past sins. After confession, the fourth part of prayer is petition, by which God is asked for great and heavenly gifts, for yourself and for all, for your relatives and friends; and, finally, conclude the prayer by giving glory to God through Christ in the Holy Spirit.[3]

John Cassian

This pattern of prayer became standard for Christian meditation, and the monk John Cassian (c. 360-435), who knew Origen's treatise, continued to comment on the prayer in a similar way. He wrote a series of *Conferences* in the form of letters addressed to Bishop Castor, Bishop Leontius and the monk Helladius, in order to help them to understand the monks under their care. These were the new monks of Gaul, and Cassian was especially involved in training those near Marseilles who wanted to follow the example of the first Christian monks. Cassian's two books, the *Institutes* and the *Conferences*, were based on his travels in Egypt, the home of early Christian monasticism, where he had talked with many of the monks in the desert. In one of the *Conferences* in particular, the ninth, which contained the second part of the teaching of Abba Isaac on prayer, Cassian commented on the Our Father. Like Origen, he saw it as containing the whole of prayer, with four stages, similar to, though not identical with, those of Origen. For Origen, the Our Father was the basic form of prayer; it has taught us that we must always seek the condition of sonship whenever we say 'Our Father'.[4] But for Cassian, the Our Father was not the limit of prayer but the beginning, the way into 'wordless prayer':

> This prayer, although it seems to contain the fullness of perfection because it was instituted and established by the authority of the Lord himself, none the less raises his friends to that condition which we characterized previously as more sublime: that fiery and wordless prayer which is known and experienced by very few.[5]

The Lord's Prayer was here seen as the gateway into mystical states of prayer, characterized by the images of fire and of tears, which the monastic tradition saw as the signs of the work of the Holy Spirit in the soul.

The Venerable Bede

In the seventh century, another monk, Bede of Wearmouth and Jarrow (673-735), also considered the Our Father to be the primary prayer for Christians among the newly-converted Anglo-Saxons in England. He did not write a treatise on the Our Father, but in his commentary on the Gospel of St Luke and in his other works on the Scriptures he referred to it constantly. Like his predecessors, Bede read more than the surface meaning of the words in every part of

5

Scripture, and this was so in his comments on the Lord's Prayer.[6] Here is an example of his method, in which he saw all parts of the Bible as one, so that part of the Old Testament can be used to illuminate the New; a sentence from the book of Samuel is connected to the gospel:

> 'Then thou [Saul] shalt go forward from thence and thou shalt come to the plain of Tabor and there shall meet thee three men going up to God at Bethel, one carrying three kids, and another carrying three loaves of bread and another carrying a bottle of wine; and they will salute thee and give thee two loaves of bread, which thou shalt receive at their hands' (1 Sam. 10: 3). The disciples received bread from the hands of the Lord when he opened their understanding that they might understand the Scriptures.[7]

Bede used the same four-fold method of understanding the Bible as his predecessors and described it under the image of cooking food in different ways:

> We are being nourished on food roasted on the gridiron when we understand literally, openly and without any covering the things that have been said or done to protect the health of the soul; we feed on food cooked in a frying-pan when, by frequently turning over the superficial meaning and looking at it afresh, we comprehend what there is in it that corresponds allegorically with the mysteries of Christ, what with the condition of the catholic church, and what with setting right the ways of individuals; and afterwards we search in the oven for the bread of the Word when by exertion of mind we lay hold of those mystical things in the Scriptures, that is, upon matters hidden above, which as yet we cannot see but which we hope we shall see hereafter.[8]

Bede also followed Origen and Cassian in presenting the Our Father as the basic structure of prayer:

> It is not without meaning that it is said that the Lord himself prayed and taught his disciples to pray, both

because the prayer he taught contained in itself the sacrament of life (and we cannot obtain the perfection of our lives except by prayer); and also because repeatedly Luke described the Saviour as praying, which prayer he carried out not for his own sake but for ours.[9]

Having established the importance of the way of prayer presented in the Our Father, Bede then discussed the whole structure of the prayer:

> In the Gospel according to Matthew the Lord's prayer seems to contain seven petitions, three of which ask for eternal things, the remaining four for things temporal, though the last four are necessary antecedents to the attainment of the eternal goods. For when we say 'Hallowed be thy name, thy kingdom come, thy will be done on earth as it is in heaven', which some understand not unfairly as in body as well as in spirit, we ask for things that are to be enjoyed for ever; they are indeed begun in this world and grow in us as we go forward, but we hope to possess them wholly in another life for ever. But when we say, 'Give us this day our daily bread, forgive us our debts as we forgive our debtors, lead us not into temptation but deliver us from evil', who does not see that these things belong to the needs of this present life? … At some services only the final part of the Lord's prayer is said aloud, and this is done so that all may reply, 'But deliver us from evil.'[10]

Bede's interest in the Lord's Prayer was not so other-worldly as that of Cassian; he allowed for an earthly meaning for the petitions, not only for the sublime heights of mysticism. He was writing for those involved in ministry to a newly-converted people and, moreover, he himself was accustomed to the daily public recitation of the Lord's Prayer in Latin as part of the Office; a section in the *Rule of St Benedict* recommends its recitation, which suggests that this was common monastic practice: 'Certainly the celebration of Lauds and Vespers must never pass by without the superior reciting the entire Lord's Prayer.'[11]

Bede was particularly concerned that this treasury of prayed theology should be available to form the structure of prayer for the whole people of God, not just for those scholars and monks who knew Latin. He wrote about this at the end of his life in his last written work, a letter to Bishop Egbert of York, an old colleague, advising him about the life of Christians in the diocese for which he was responsible. Bede stressed the importance of seeing that the Our Father was known by heart by all, in English where Latin was not known:

> In preaching to the people, this message more than any other should be proclaimed; that the catholic faith as contained in the Apostles' Creed and the Lord's Prayer, which the reading of the gospel teaches us, should be interiorly memorized by all who are under your rule. All who have learnt Latin by constant reading have certainly learnt these texts as well, but as for the unlearned, that is, those who know only their own tongue, let them learn the texts in their own language and sing them accurately. This should be done not only by the laity, who are still living a worldly life, but also by any clerks and monks who are not expert in the Latin language. So it will come about that the whole congregation of believers will learn how to be full of faith and will know how to protect and arm themselves against the attacks of evil spirits by firm belief. The result will be that the whole choir of those who are praying to God will understand what should be specially sought from the mercy of God. That is why I have often made translations of both the Creed and the Lord's Prayer into English and offered them to priests who do not know Latin. ... Moreover, the custom of repeated prayer and genuflexions has taught us to sing the Lord's Prayer more often.[12]

No translations of the Our Father by Bede into Anglo-Saxon are extant; but there are later versions that must have been very close to his work, and they show how the text could be presented faithfully but at the same time given meaning in phrases familiar to a new culture. This version is a brief commentary on each clause of the prayer; the main version which was known by heart would have been shorter.

Pater noster qui es in celis

Father of mankind, I pray you for healing, holy Lord in the heavens.

sanctificetur nomen tuum.

May this your name be hallowed now, fast fixed in our minds, redeeming Christ, fast established in our hearts.

Adveniat regnum tuum.

May your kingdom now come to us mortals, Wielder of mighty powers, righteous Judge, and may your glorious faith remain in our hearts for the span of our lives.

Fiat voluntas tua sicut in celo et in terra.

And may your will be fulfilled among us in the habitation of the kingdom of earth, as clear as it is in the glory of heaven, made both dear and lovely for ever and to eternity.

Panem nostrum cotidianum da nobis hodie

Give us now today, Lord of men, high King of the heavens, our bread, which you sent into the world as salvation to the souls of mankind: that is, the pure Christ, the Lord God.

et dimitte nobis debita nostra

Forgive us, Guardian of men, our guilts and sins, and pardon our crimes, the body's wounds, and our wicked deeds, although we often offend against you, the almighty God, in your mercies,

sicut et nos dimittimus debitoribus nostris.

just as we pardon on earth the crimes of those who often do wrong against us, and do not think to accuse them of their evil deeds, in order to have eternal life.

9

Et ne nos inducas in temptationem

Do not lead us to punishment, to the grief of affliction, nor to the testing, redeeming Christ, lest we, devoid of grace, become out of enmity estranged from all your mercies.

sed libera nos a malo.

And also free us now from the evil of every fiend; we in our hearts shall eagerly speak of thanks and glory, Prince of the angels, true Lord of victories, because you have mercifully set us free from the bondage of hell's torments by your mighty power.

Amen.

So let it be.[13]

It was the content and inner meaning of the prayer that was to be known, not just external words; it was therefore to be said in a familiar language and also given the extra dignity of being sung by all. This advice was echoed later when Alfred the Great began to reconstruct the English Church and nation after the incursions of the Danes, and he attributed the failure of the late Anglo-Saxon Church to its not having followed this advice of Bede about seeing that the content of the prayer was absorbed through the use of translations:

Before everything was ransacked and burned, the churches throughout England were filled with treasures and with books. Similarly, there was a great multitude serving God. They derived very little benefit from their books because they could understand nothing of them since they were not written in their own language. Therefore we have now lost the wealth as well as the wisdom, because we did not wish to set our minds on the right way.[14]

Alcuin of York

Fifty years later this approach was paralleled by another Anglo-Saxon scholar, Alcuin of York (736-804). A devoted admirer of Bede, Alcuin was an Englishman who had been taught by Bede's pupil and colleague Egbert of York. He became Master of the Cathedral School at York and was later the central figure in the Carolingian renaissance at the court of Charlemagne. Like Bede he included in his comments on the Lord's Prayer the passage already quoted from Bede on the form of the prayer, but in his comments clause by clause he was concerned with content and meaning for the praying heart. While Bede's comments are embedded in biblical exposition and homilies, Alcuin's commentary is found in the part of his work that deals with the liturgical prayer of the Church, thus giving it a corporate setting as the central prayer for Christians when they pray together.[15] Together, Bede and Alcuin presented the interior understanding of the Lord's Prayer for the English as being essential, whether prayed alone or with others.

Teresa of Avila

In the sixteenth century, there was another notable exposition of the Lord's Prayer by Teresa of Avila (1515-97). The founder of the Order of Discalced Carmelites, and the first woman to be given the title Doctor of the Church, she was the contemplative writer *par excellence*. She was most concerned with the exploration of prayer as a way of life, which might or might not include mystical states of prayer, and she wrote her work on the Our Father in Spanish for her nuns while she was at her new foundation of St Joseph's. At the request of these enclosed contemplative nuns, she wrote about the way of prayer they were following, concentrating in *The Way of Perfection* on vocal prayer that was common to all, and drawing from it the highest levels of contemplation. The heart of the treatise (chapters 27-42; fifteen chapters out of forty-two) analyses the Our Father; these chapters are sometimes printed separately and called the *Paternoster Treatise*.[16] For Teresa, the specific nature of Christian prayer began with the gift of God in his Son; the beginning was not the creation but the re-creation of all. She exclaims at the wonder of this claim of sonship in the first words of the prayer, given that it is the end and aim and height of perfection. She suggests that it might seem more appropriate to start at the end, with 'Deliver us from evil', since the phrase 'Our Father' is in a sense the climax of prayer rather than the beginning.[17] She also, like Origen and Cassian, saw it as being prayed by Jesus himself, as his prayer to the Father; and she goes even further than her predecessors in explaining how the whole way of mystical union is contained within it:

> The heavenly perfection of this evangelical prayer is something for which we should give great praise to the Lord. It was so well composed by the good Master, my daughters, that each of us may use it in her own way. I am astounded when I consider that in its few words are contained the whole of contemplation and perfection, so that if we study it no other book will be necessary. In the Paternoster the Lord has taught us the whole method of prayer and contemplation, from the first beginnings of mental prayer to the prayerful states of Quiet and Union.[18]

Summary

The approach of all these writers is similar; their understanding of the Our Father is that it is primarily the prayer of Jesus praying to the Father and including in his words all created beings as sons in the Son. Within this new relationship, established by redemption, the whole of prayer can be found in these words, and the prayer itself can also be a basis for the way of mystical and contemplative union with God. Each of these writers makes specific comments on the separate clauses of the Our Father, some of which I have grouped together under each phrase, to offer a sense of the interpretation most often given to the separate sections.

DETAILED COMMENTS

Our Father

Each of the commentators begins with the statement that the fatherhood of God is conferred not only by creation but by the adoption of humanity in the second person of the Trinity, the Son of God:

> When we confess with our own voice that the God and Father of the universe is Our Father, we are affirming that we have in fact been taken out of our servile condition and given sonship by adoption.[19]

This is presented as true whenever the prayer is said, but especially so when it is used in the context of the Eucharist:

> And here the priest joins his hands and says 'Let us pray', and the church prays with the priest not in voice but in heart. In silence the heart cries to God in the ears of God, 'Our Father'. The only begotten Son has made us sons of God by the font of new birth and the spirit of adoption. So when we do what he says, 'When you pray, say, "Our Father", we are acting out of obedience, not out of boldness. The sons must imitate their good father as Isaac imitated Abraham and Jacob [imitated] Isaac, as he said: "Be ye holy because I the LORD your God am holy"' (Lev. 20: 26).[20]

The idea of God as a loving and present Father, who cares intimately for his children, follows from this:

> You have a good Father given you by the good Jesus; let no other father be known or referred to here. Strive, my daughters, to be such that you deserve to find comfort in him and to throw yourselves into his arms. You know that, if you are good children, he will never send you away.[21]

Who art in heaven

The second clause of the prayer, again in the present tense, affirms that 'our Father' is eternally present beyond the confines and limitations of this earthly life, not somewhere different in space but in the 'heaven' of an eternal now; the response to this realization is therefore stated in terms of a dynamic pilgrimage to him:

> Avoid with utter horror staying in the dwelling-place of this present life; here we live on earth as on a journey and are kept at a far distance from our Father. Let us instead hasten with great desire to that region in which we say that our Father dwells.[22]

The idea of life as a pilgrimage, a journey to the place where we really belong, does not locate 'heaven' as always ahead; heaven is also within the soul of everyone created in the image and likeness of God, so that God is always within us, for intimate converse:

> We have no need to go to heaven or to speak in a loud voice; however quietly we speak he is so near that he will hear us. ... There are those who are able to shut themselves up in this way within this little heaven of the soul wherein dwells the Maker of heaven and earth; they will come without fail to drink of the water of the fountain of life.[23]

Hallowed be thy name

The prayer that the name of God may be known as holy is linked by all writers with the service of Christians, in whom Christ lives and acts:

> Hallowed be thy name—this is done by self-giving service by Christ in us for the sake of all. We testify that our desire and joy is the glory of the Father, since we have become imitators of him who said: 'The one who speaks of himself seeks his own glory, but the one who seeks the glory of him who sent him is true and there is no unrighteousness in him' (John 7: 18).[24]

The question of any incongruity in asking for something that already exists, since the name of God is by definition holy, is resolved by underlining the continuing hallowing of the earthly life of Christians, as they strive always to become what they already are:

> The name of God is holy, so why do we say, 'Hallowed be thy name'? When we are born again by water and the Spirit at baptism, we are made holy in the name of God almighty when the priest says, 'I baptize you in the name of the Father and of the Son and of the Holy Spirit'. So we pray that the holiness that was created in us then at baptism by the invocation of God may fill us for ever so that we may not corrupt it; but, just as we were once made holy, so we may remain so for all eternity. Let us understand how holy thy Name is, that is, it is holy in all things and when we remember such holiness we should be afraid to sin. If anyone is a good Christian he does good work, so that in this way the name of Christ is hallowed in his servants; we pray that the name of God may be made holy by being praised and glorified in all our works. For whatever we do that is good is for his praise but whatever we do that is bad brings scorn upon him.[25]

Such a 'hallowing' of those who pray is, therefore, a hallowing of all creation, by returning everything made to a right relationship with its creator. Such a redeeming work must be constantly worked for, but it is a gift of God which must also be asked for:

> Make us such, Father, that we may deserve to understand and grasp how great your hallowing is … that you may appear as hallowed in our hallowed way of life.[26]

Thy kingdom come

The next clause also relates to heaven, and is a prayer that the kingdom of God will come, which is seen as both a prayer for the indwelling of heaven in each soul now, but also as a prayer of longing for the total rule of Christ on earth:

Desire the heavens to be now and within us. Christ reigns daily in those who pray when the rule of the devil has been cast out of their hearts and God has begun to hold sway.[27]

But this also raises the question of unanswered prayer, since the kingdom does not seem to have come, however often it is prayed for. In a sense there is no such thing as unanswered prayer; the dimension of time is not the same as the eternity of God, where all prayer is granted; on earth, the answer is always 'yes', but not always in the way expected or at the time it is asked:

> It also sometimes happens that we seek things entirely related to salvation with our eager petitions and right actions and yet we do not immediately obtain what we ask. The result of our petitions is postponed to some future time, as when we daily ask the Father on bended knees, saying, 'Thy kingdom come'; we are not going to receive the kingdom as soon as our prayer is finished but at the proper time.[28]

Though this is true, in another sense the 'kingdom' is seen as already being given to those who ask for it:

> What is the kingdom of God? Eternal blessedness, as it is said, 'Come, ye blessed of my Father' (Matt. 25: 34). The almighty God reigns in his chosen ones by faith, hope and love and all good works; the devil reigns in us by greed, drunkenness, hatred and all evils; so we pray that it may be the Lord who reigns in us by righteousness and not the devil by sin.[29]

The journey of prayer towards the Father in heaven is life-long, but it may contain times when the peace of the kingdom is experienced as a present reality:

> We are making a sea-voyage and are still on the journey. But there are times when we are wearied with travelling and the Lord grants tranquillity to our senses and quiet to our souls; this prayer of quiet is a foretaste of the kingdom for which we pray continually.[30]

Thy will be done on earth as it is in heaven

The next clause, that the will of God may be done on earth as it is already done in heaven, is a reminder that the angels, who always behold the face of God, perfectly do his will; but also that, for human beings, the will of God is summed up in the word 'redemption':

> The will of God is the salvation of all … in other words, we are saying, 'Father, just as those in heaven are saved by knowing you, so also are those who are on earth'.[31]

It is also a reminder that the will of God is not to be confused with the will of the person praying; for, however clear it is to the petitioners that what they ask is right, there is no guarantee that this is so:

> We are admonished to include in the Lord's Prayer, 'Thy will be done', that is, not our own. For if we remember as well that saying of the apostle, 'We do not know what to pray for as we ought' (Rom. 8: 26), we shall understand that sometimes we beg for things opposed to our salvation and are very appropriately denied these things that we ask for earnestly by him who knows what is right for us more truly than we do.[32]

The will of God is being done on earth by continual prayer for the indwelling of Christ:

> In heaven the angels who never sinned do your will and their service is always acceptable to you; so let your good will be done on earth so that your servants may be pleasing to you. By heaven we understand the Lord Jesus Christ, by earth, the church. We know that as a man is to a woman, so is heaven to earth. From heaven the church receives all its fruitfulness, 'every good and perfect gift cometh from above' (Jas 1: 17). Just as your will is done in heaven, which is Christ, so may it be done in the church, which is his body. As it is done in the heaven of just men, so may it be done also in the earth of sinners by their repentance.[33]

Give us this day our daily bread

The next clause links heaven and earth, the petitions connected with heaven to those concerned with earthly matters. This link is Christ, seen as the bread of life, which is love:

> Give us this bread as long as we live on earth … we beg you to give it us today because unless we receive it in this life, we shall not be ready to receive it in the life to come.[34]

Though one meaning of the 'bread' must be the 'eucharistic bread', another and equally valid meaning, and one emphasized in the early Church, was that it meant the Scriptures, which were broken open when they were read:

> By breaking the bread which he gave to his disciples, the Lord designates the opening of the secret meanings by which the world was to be nourished unto perpetual salvation. We cannot ourselves penetrate to the inner meaning of the bread of life, but true understanding of it will be opened to us by him.[35]

To ask for this bread of love is always to receive it:

> We must not fear that, if we seek the gift of love from the Lord with deep devotion and say from the depth of our hearts, 'Give us today our daily bread', he will let our hearts be narrowed into the rigidity of hatred.[36]

This daily bread has also a natural meaning and includes what is needed to sustain earthly life, as well as being a request with a deeper meaning:

> Give us this day our daily bread: bread means all that is necessary for us in food, drink, clothing, to be given us today in this temporal life. By daily bread we can understand the body and blood of Christ of which he said, 'Unless you eat of this bread' (John 6: 54). Let us pray that in receiving his body and his blood, by that which we see with our eyes we may receive that which we do not see, that is, almighty God: 'whoso eateth my flesh and drinketh my blood remains in me and I in him' (John 6: 51).

Where it says 'daily', perhaps we think we cannot be referring to the reception of communion, since there are those who think they cannot receive it daily because of sin. There are others, however, who do so, remembering that the Lord said to Zacchaeus, 'Today I must stay in your house', and he received him joyfully (Luke 19: 5). Those who feel they cannot do this are saying with the centurion, 'Lord, I am not worthy to receive you under my roof' (Matt. 8: 8) and they are adding by implication, 'I will come another day'. But Augustine says of this kind of humility, 'Brothers, I am pleased with your humility in fearing to receive the body and blood of the Lord, but it would be better if you were to receive it as cleansing for your sins and as repentance.' By bread we also understand the word of God speaking in the law, the prophets, the Psalms and the Gospels. In the time of our mortal life, refresh us with the teaching of the holy Scriptures, so that, as our body is refreshed by earthly food, so this spiritual food may refresh our souls to love and knowledge of you.[37]

The prayer for bread is to be offered daily, until life opens out into the great and ultimate day of the Lord:

He who today prays to God, who is from infinity to infinity, not only for this day but for each day, will be ready to receive from him even greater things.[38]

And forgive us our trespasses,
as we forgive those who trespass against us

In this section of the prayer, repentance and sorrow for sin predominate. The severe note of reality reminds us that those who do not forgive cannot themselves be forgiven, not because of any arbitrary refusal by God, but because only by forgiving can the heart be ready to receive forgiveness:

If we want to be judged mercifully we must ourselves be merciful to those who have offended us, for we shall be forgiven to the degree that we have forgiven those who have injured us by any wrongdoing whatsoever.[39]

Such forgiveness is always necessary, even for those who have been baptized:

> Whoever has been cleansed in the baptismal font and has received pardon for sins has no need to be cleansed again, and, moreover, cannot be cleansed again in the same way. It is necessary only to have the daily defilements of worldly life wiped away by the daily forgiveness of the Redeemer. The whole body together with its actions is clean, with the exception only of those things that cling to the mind because of temporal cares. It is for cleansing from daily defilement that we say daily in prayer, 'forgive us our trespasses as we forgive those who trespass against us'.[40]

It is not only by doing wrong actions that the soul is blinded by sin; it is also by failing to do good:

> We are debtors to God in two ways, either by doing what he has forbidden or by not doing what he has commanded. Do we love God and our neighbour as he commanded? We are debtors, sinners. Do we honour our parents? We are debtors and sinners. Do not kill, do not commit adultery, do not swear, do not give false witness: we are daily offending against what he has commanded and so we are his debtors. If we would be forgiven by the Lord we must forgive others from the heart; or else we are doubly disobedient both by our own sins and by not loving our neighbour as we are commanded, since we do not forgive. He who taught us to pray about our offences and sins promised that his fatherly mercy and pardon would follow us ... In this life he forgives our daily and individual sins, without which we cannot live in this life (1 John 1: 7).[41]

There is here an awareness of the dialectic of being and becoming; the death and resurrection of Christ have redeemed humanity in one cosmic event, but each person had still to appropriate freely that fact into himself or herself, and this is therefore a continual request:

The blood of Jesus his Son cleanses us from all sins. For the sacrament of the Lord's passion has equally freed us from all sin in baptism and the grace of our Redeemer forgives whatever we have committed through daily frailty after baptism. With humility we daily confess our errors to him when we receive the sacrament of his blood. After forgiving those who trespass against us, we entreat that our trespasses be forgiven us, praying that, mindful of his passion, we may gladly bear all adversities.[42]

Loving-kindness, good intentions, forgetting rather than forgiving, are never enough; the forgiveness that is being sought here is a deeper aspect of the fire of charity, which is God, and which includes truth as well as love:

Charity covers a multitude of sins, especially when someone says truthfully to God, 'forgive us our trespasses as we forgive those who trespass against us'. And indeed all good works that we profess wipe away and cover the faults we commit, but this is said particularly about the charity by which we give to our neighbours those things that were given to us, because it is just in the sight of God that it be measured out to us according to the measure of devotion that we have ourselves measured.[43]

It is necessary, therefore, to be able to realize that salvation is dependent not just on interior and personal sorrow but upon the practical matter of the attitude each has towards others:

O Almighty God, just as we forgive those who have sinned against us, do you forgive us. If we have not forgiven them, do not forgive our sins against you, as it is said, 'if you do not forgive, neither will my Father forgive you your sins' (Matt. 7: 15).[44]

And lead us not into temptation

This is a clause about self-knowledge, as well as one that affirms the place of humility in life. Temptations are seen as having a positive role in life, enabling clarity and understanding of the self in all its weakness and showing to what depths it is capable of falling:

> The gifts our soul has received are unknown to everyone except God. They are unknown even to ourselves. Through temptations, they become known. Thereafter we cannot be ignorant of what we are, for we know ourselves ... and we look to the future and prepare ourselves against what may befall us.[45]

But, aware of the weakness within, that God allows to continue out of his infinite respect for freedom, we also need to ask that such knowledge may not be too much to be borne:

> Do not allow us to be tried by the devil beyond our capacity, but with the trial also 'provide a way by which we may endure' (1 Cor. 10: 13).[46]

Temptation can be seen as the spurious attraction of evil for weakness, and, because of this meaning of 'temptation', it is proper to ask that it may not be too overwhelming to resist. But 'temptation' can also be seen as something allowed by God, who does not override free will; in which case such testing can be seen as a chance to increase in strength of commitment to Christ. The way of growing up to the full measure of maturity in Christ is not an easy gift of God given once for all, but a vital part of existence:

> There is one kind of temptation that is a testing, as God tempted Abraham to prove his faith; there is another temptation that is of the devil, for 'God tempts no one' (Jas. 1: 13). We pray not to be led into the devil's temptation beyond what our frailty is able to bear. God is said to lead us into temptation when he does not free us from temptation.[47]

But deliver us from evil

The prayer for delivery out of all evil is most earnestly commented on, since in life there is always the possibility of failure. Its seriousness is underlined by commentators who illuminate it by using the imagery of battles, of soldiers, of fighting, which has been used in this connection from the first century to today:

> The soldiers of Christ—namely those who are learning contemplation and practising prayer—are always ready for the hour of conflict. They are never very much afraid of their open enemies, for they know who they are and are sure that they cannot prevail against the strength given them by the Lord … Those whom they fear and fear rightly, and from whom they always ask the Lord to deliver them, are enemies who are treacherous, devils who transform themselves and visit them disguised as angels of light.[48]

There is no permanent deliverance from the condition of being human during life on earth, and so this prayer continues to be needed:

> The whole life of man on earth is temptation. Let us pray to be delivered from temptation, not that we should not be tempted, which is impossible for those on earth, but that we may not yield when we are tempted.[49]

Amen

This word contains echoes of the earliest forms of Christian liturgy, when all the congregation, according to third-century writers, united in the great 'amen' at the end of the central prayer of the Eucharist: 'So be it' is said to signify and confirm this prayer. "For thine is the kingdom and the power and the glory for ever and ever."'

It is a final affirmation that whatever has been said was truly meant:

> 'Amen' is the seal set on this prayer, like a seal that confirms a legal document. It is as if those who say this more especially confirm that last clause, saying, 'Indeed, what I have said I meant. If I have forgiven those who have sinned against me, forgive me whatever I have done against you; but if I have not forgiven, neither should you forgive me.'[50]

Conclusion

These comments on the Our Father are based on the premise that it is a prayer that at once links those praying into the relationship of Christ to the Father, and, since it is plural, with all others, as children of God; they therefore become part of the eternal love between Father and Son, which is the Holy Spirit. This sonship is not remote; it is not a matter of undertaking severe training to attain prayer at the end of a hard road. It is given at once, in the present tense, now and available for use. It is prayer that already exists and can be entered into. It is for all—for Tatiana and Ambrose, a married and elderly couple in the church of the martyrs; for the new monks of Gaul, converted barbarians who wanted their lives to be based on the traditions of the desert monks of Egypt; for the energetic but unlearned new Christians of Anglo-Saxon England; for a small group of middle-class young ladies of northern Spain, who were becoming nuns just when the Reformation was happening in Northern Europe. These were not theologians or academics, or specially educated—just people baptized and serious about a life of prayer. The Our Father is available for all, since it is not separate from the doctrines of creation, redemption and sanctification. The text is a door through which we enter and 'go in' with Christ to the father and 'go out' to all creation and so 'find pasture'.

The shape of the Paternoster is consistent with all prayer. It has two parts: the first begins in heaven and is linked to the second, earthly needs, by bread, which is Christ, who is love. The Our Father gives the outline and pattern for all prayer, and the more it is repeated the more it becomes physically part of those who use it, by being contained in the memory; and therefore the more it is absorbed, the more the commandment is fulfilled to 'pray without ceasing' (1 Thess. 5: 17). It can continue as prayer silently contained within the heart, so that the Christian who is among other people is always saying for them with Christ, 'Our Father'.

Basic as it is to Christianity, nevertheless the Our Father is not a ritual formula that can produce a result, nor is it a prayer that has to be used. Each author cited sees it, not as a limiting straitjacket, but as a working pattern by which Christians enter into prayer in the Spirit, which is the dynamic life of love in the Trinity. It provides a guaranteed way into the life of God, but God is always larger than his own rules. To underline this I will end with a quotation from Tolstoy's story, 'The Three Old Men'. He describes three very old men who had lived on a remote island, unknown all their lives. They received a visit from an archbishop, who asked them how they prayed; they told him that all they ever said was: 'You are three and we are three; have mercy on us.'

Slightly scandalized, the archbishop patiently taught them, word by word, the scriptural prayer of the Our Father, and left them saying it. But in the night, as his ship sailed away, he saw a light following the ship:

He saw the three old men running on the sea, their grey beards showing dazzlingly white, their feet overhauling the ship as though it had been standing still.

When the old men reached the ship they raised their heads above the side and said they had forgotten the Lord's Prayer and asked to be taught it again.

But the archbishop said: 'Your prayer too, O ancient men of God, was profitable unto the Lord. It is not for me to teach you. Pray you rather for us sinners.' And the archbishop bowed to his feet before the old men. For a moment they stood motionless—then turned and went back across the sea and until morning a light could be seen glowing in the direction in which they had departed.[51]

NOTES

[1] Origen, *On Prayer*, ch. 2. (hereafter 'Origen'). (Translations of ancient sources throughout this book are by Benedicta Ward.)

[2] Origen, ch. 18.

[3] Origen, ch. 33.

[4] John Cassian, *Conferences*, Conference 9: 'Abba Isaac On Prayer', 18.2 (hereafter 'Cassian').

[5] Cassian, 25.1.

[6] Bede, *Commentary on Luke*, in *Bedae Venerabilis Opera*, CCSL CXX, ed. D. Hurst (Turnholt, Brepols, 1960), pp. 229-230.

[7] Bede, *Commentary on Samuel*, in *Bedae Venerabilis Opera*, CCSL CX1X, ed. D. Hurst (Turnholt, Brepols, 1969), p. 87.

[8] Bede, *Samuel*, pp. 815-24.

[9] Bede, *Luke*, p. 227.

[10] Bede, *Luke*, p. 227.

[11] *Rule of St Benedict*, ch. 13.

[12] Bede, 'Letter to Egbert'.

[13] Anglo-Saxon Our Father, Worcester, c. 1000, Oxford Bodleian Library Ms Junius 121, fol. 43 (alternative version in *Anglo-Saxon Poetry*, tr. S. A. J. Bradley, Everyman's Library, London, Dent, 1982).

[14] Alfred the Great, his preface to his translation of Gregory the Great's *Pastoral Care*.

[15] Alcuin, *Liber de Divinis Officiis*, PL 101:1265Ff. (hereafter 'Alcuin').

[16] Teresa of Avila, *The Way of Perfection*, ch. xxvii–xlii (hereafter 'Teresa').

[17] For a similar approach, cf. Anthony Bloom, 'Living Prayer', in *The Essence of Prayer* (Darton, Longman & Todd, 1986), pp. 18-19.

[18] Teresa, ch. xxxvii.

[19] Cassian, xviii.2.

[20] Bede, *Commentaries on the Catholic Epistles*, in *Bedae Venerabilis Opera*, CCSL CXXI, ed. D. Hurst (Turnholt, Brepols, 1962), 1 Pet. 1: 16, p. 75.

[21] Teresa, ch. xxvii.

[22] Cassian, xx.11.

[23] Teresa, ch. xxviii.

[24] Cassian, xviii.5.

[25] Alcuin, col. 1266B.

[26] Cassian, viii.5.

[27] Origen, ch. 25.

[28] Bede, *Homilies*, 'Sermon after Easter' 11.12, in *Bedae Venerabilis Opera Homiletica*, CCSL CXXII, ed. D. Hurst (Turnholt, Brepols, 1955), p. 261 (hereafter '*Homilies*').

[29] Alcuin, col. 1266D.

[30] Teresa, ch. xxx.

[31] Cassian, xx.2.

[32] Bede, *Homilies*, 'Sermon at the Greater Litanies', 2.14, p. 277.

[33] Alcuin, cols. 1266D-1267A.

[34] Cassian, 21.2.

[35] Bede, *Commentary on Mark*, in *Bedae Venerabilis Opera*, CCSL CXXII, ed. D. Hurst (Turnholt, Brepols, 1955), p. 529.

[36] Bede, *Homilies*, 'Sermon at the Greater Litanies', 11.14, p. 131.

[37] Alcuin, cols 1267C-1268B.

[38] Origen, ch. 27.16.

[39] Cassian, xxii.2.

[40] Bede, *Homilies*, 'Homily for Holy Thursday', 11.5, p. 217.

[41] Alcuin, col. 1268D.

[42] Bede, *Homilies*, 'Sermon at the Greater Litanies', 11. 14, p. 273.

[43] Bede, 'On the Catholic Epistles', in *Bedae Venerabilis Opera*, CCSL CXXI, ed. D. Hurst (Turnholt, Brepols, 1955), 1 Pet. 4, p. 110.

[44] Alcuin, col. 1268D.

[45] Origen, ch. 29.17.

[46] Cassian, xxiii.1.

[47] Alcuin, col. 1267D.

[48] Teresa, ch. xxxviii.

[49] Origen, ch. 29.9.

[50] Alcuin, col. 1269B.

[51] Leo Tolstoy, 'The Three Hermits', in *Master and Man and Other Parables and Tales,* (Everyman's Library; London, J. M. Dent & Sons; New York, E. P. Dutton & Co.), p. 180.

SOURCES IN ENGLISH TRANSLATION

Alfred the Great, Preface to his translation of Gregory's *Pastoral Care*, in *Alfred the Great*, tr. Simon Keynes and Michael Lapidge (Harmondsworth, Penguin Books, 1983).

Bede, *Homilies on the Gospels*, tr. L. Martin and D. Hurst, 2 vols., (Cistercian Studies; Kalamazoo, MI, Cistercian Publications, 1991).

Bede, 'Letter to Egbert', in *Ecclesiastical History of the English People*, tr. J. McClure (Oxford, Oxford University Press, 2000).

Cassian, John, *Conferences*, tr. Boniface Ramsey (Ancient Christian Writers; New York, Paulist Press, 1997).

Origen, *On Prayer*, tr. John J. O'Meara (Ancient Christian Writers; New York, Newman Press, 1954).

Teresa of Avila, 'The Way of Perfection', in *The Complete Works of Saint Teresa of Jesus*, vol. 2, tr. E. Allison Peers (London, Sheed and Ward, 1949).